3 Day Guide to Cinque Terre

A 72-hour definitive guide on what to see, eat and enjoy in Cinque Terre, Italy

3 DAY CITY GUIDES

Cover Images

Santa Margherita d'Antiochia, Vernazza. Photo by <u>Pank Seelen</u>

Homework. Photo by <u>Katri Niemi</u>

Riomaggiore. Photo by <u>François Philipp</u>

Monterosso. Photo by <u>ccharmon</u>

ISBN: 1515179540

ISBN-13: 978-1515179542

"Our battered suitcases were piled on the sidewalk again; we had longer ways to go. But no matter, the road is life." – Jack Kerouac

CONTENTS

1   Introduction to Cinque Terre   7

2   Cinque Terre Neighborhoods   26

3   How to Not Get Lost in Cinque Terre   30

4   Day 1 in Cinque Terre   32

5   Day 2 in Cinque Terre   37

6   Day 3 in Cinque Terre   42

7   Local Cuisine in Cinque Terre   48

8   Where To Dine   51

9   Best Places to Unwind   55

10   Where to Stay in Cinque Terre   57

11   Cinque Terre Travel Essentials   60

12   Top Things to Do in Cinque Terre   64

13   Italian Language Essentials   69

Conclusion   75

More from This Author

1 INTRODUCTION TO CINQUE TERRE

Vernazza, Cinque Terre. Photo by Daniel Stockman

Located in northern Italy between Pisa and Genoa lies the Italian Riviera---a sun-kissed coastal region that may be as pure as any place gets. This is not an overrun tourist destination, but more a sleepy place of sand, sea, wine and lazy days.

That's not to say it hasn't been discovered. It would be hard to keep such a beautiful place a secret. But it's blessedly low key, with a lack of cars and very few major tourist attractions or corporate development. It won't be long until you're feeling as relaxed as the breeze when you visit.

It wasn't long ago that the five towns that make up this region were poor and remote—as hard as it might be to believe. Today, it is connected to the rest of Italy by trains and it's this ease of access that has buffeted the region's popularity. What makes it special, though, still lingers in its traditions, its food, and the proud heritage of each village you encounter.

And you won't be the only ones to declare this place special. In an effort to preserve Cinque Terre's natural wonders, Italy declared the entire region to be a park, and it was crowned as a UNESCO World Heritage Site in 1997. As you walk from town to town, you'll no doubt discover why.

The Roman's thought it was special too, but certainly not for the sunbathing. Where there was water, there were Romans and the coastline in this region played an important role in the empire. In the 14th century, though, the Saracens came to occupy the region and the locals ran to the hills when their towns were destroyed.

It was the Tuscan Obertengo family that restored Cinque Terre to its former glory. They ousted the Saracens and encouraged local tribes to move back to the sea where the first houses were built. They put "Italian" back into the region by building stone walls, planting olive and lemon trees and grape vines and turning rough mountain slopes into terraces for planting. Watchtowers helped to keep pirates and barbarians at bay, and commerce on the sea started in earnest.

It wasn't long before the region became known for its wine. But it was also known for its excellent defenses. In the 16th century, pirates lodged many attacks against the Ligurian Coast (another name for the area) but the villages held strong. In years to come, they'd face a host of natural disasters that would see the population drop, but in the end, their excellent wine always saved the day.

The unification of Italy in the 1800's was a boon to the area when trains were built that pointed in the direction of the coast. In 1960, when the coastal road was paved, it beckoned tourists who came for the amazing views overlooking the villages and the sea. Travel writers brought even more crowds, and today Cinque Terre is sharing its charms with the rest of the world. It may just boast some of the most beautiful scenery in the world.

Climate and Seasons

Thanks to the Apennine Mountains, the climate of the Liguria coast tends to be mild. The mountains bring much-needed relief in the form of north winds to the hot, humid summers. Anything that clears humidity from the air in an Italian summer is a welcome treat. The lack of humidity also clears the air, providing great views up and down the coast.

The summers also tend to be dry---which isn't only great for the tourists, but also great for the grapes. The dry days help to concentrate the flavor of the grapes that grow along the terraced hillsides where hikers traverse between the five villages.

It rains the most in spring and fall and for people who plan on hiking, this might be a deterrent. But despite the threat of rain, April and May in Cinque Terre can be quite nice and it's a favorite time of year for many people who visit Italy often.

The summer is undoubtedly the busiest time of year along the Ligurian Coast, with Italians taking their holidays and tourists who come from around the world to play during the summer holiday season. Many are day-trippers from nearby Florence or Genoa. The hottest months are July and August when temperatures can top off in the high 80s or low 90s.

Temperatures cool in the autumn, and many people say that September and October are the perfect time to visit. The days are often sunny with cooler nights.

While there can be sunny days in the winters months, this seaside region can get quite cold in the winter. Even so, some travelers prefer the offseason for its lack of tourists and quiet trails. And in the midst of winter, there's no denying that Cinque Terre is still a beautiful place.

The offseason is from mid-September to mid-June, excluding Easter.

Take a look at the average temperatures in Cinque Terre by the month:

January: **High** 50 °F (10 °C), **Low** 34 °F (1 °C)

February: **High** 53 °F (12 °C), **Low** 37 °F (3 °C)

March: **High** 59 °F (15 °C), **Low** 40 °F (4 °C)

April: **High** 65 °F (18 °C), **Low** 45 °F (7 °C)

May: **High** 74 °F (23 °C), **Low** 52 °F (11 °C)

June: **High** 81 °F (27 °C), **Low** 58 °F (14 °C)

July: **High** 88 °F (31 °C), **Low** 63 °F (17 °C)

August: **High** 87 °F (31 °C), **Low** 62 °F (17 °C)

September: **High** 79 °F (26 °C), **Low** 57 °F (14 °C)

October: **High** 70 °F (21 °C), **Low** 50 °F (10 °C)

November: **High** 58 °F (14 °C), **Low** 41 °F (5 °C)

December: **High** 50 °F (10 °C), **Low** 36 °F (2 °C)

When to Visit

During the summer months, the five tiny, seaside towns that make up Cinque Terre are filled to the brim with visitors. Accommodations are hard to find if they're not booked in advance, and the narrow streets and famous hiking paths are crowded with tourists. That's not to say that visiting the area during the busy season isn't recommended. Just make sure you prepare in advance while also remaining cognizant of the fact that you will be sharing your trip with a slew of other tourists.

Visiting the towns outside of high season is highly recommended if you're looking for a less hectic introduction to the region. And as much as possible, it's best to visit when the threat of rain is lowest. And not just because the spectacular scenery is not to be missed, but also because hiking (the top activity as the trails traverse to each of the five towns) can be difficult during the rainy season. The hiking paths can close if the weather is inclement. Sometimes sections of the paths wash away, forcing an entire route to close until it can be repaired. Even if it has rained recently, it may take a while to reopen closed paths.

Having said that, it is impossible to predict the weather. In a perfect world, you'd pick a season in which to visit and the weather would be sunny and beautiful each and every day. The schedules of many people dictate when they travel, so go to Cinque Terre when you can and hope for good weather. Keep in mind there are trains that bring visitors from town to town, and you can alter your vacation plans by using the trains if hiking from town to town is difficult.

Outside of high season, two of the best months to visit are May and October. There are fewer visitors, less rain and plenty enough sun.

Winter can be cold and some of the shops and restaurants close down this time of year. The good news is that prices are lower and there are fewer tourists. Be sure to dress in layers and pack warm clothes if you visit this time of year. Also, prepare to be flexible about your plans---especially hiking.

The driest weather is in July when an average of 1.1 inch of rainfall occurs.

The wettest weather is in October when an average of 6 inches of rainfall occurs.

Here is the region's average precipitation by month:

January: 4.1 inches

February: 3.7inches

March: 4.2 inches

April: 3.4 inches

May: 3.0 inches

June: 2.1 inches

July: 1.1 inches

August: 3.2 inches

September: 3.0 inches

October: 6.0 inches

November: 4.3 inches

December: 2.2 inches

Language

It's a good idea to get to know the language of any country you intend to visit—even if it's just a few words or phrases. The good news is that Italian is a beautiful, poetic language and it's not too hard to learn some simple words. It evolved from the vernacular of ancient Rome and has a fascinating transformative history.

Europe was once a pandemonium of endless dialects derived from Latin, and Italy was no exception, since it was made up of different city states. It was hard for a merchant in Florence to communicate with a business owner from Rome.

But when Italian unification became a reality in 1861, it was clear that the country needed one decisive language. Italian intellectuals gathered and chose Florence's dialect as Italy's official language. And which Florentine dialect did they settle on? The one spoken by the great poet Dante Alighieri.

It's also a good idea to buy a small language book (or use the language guide included) you can carry around with you that translates Italian words to English and vice versa, or download one to your smart phone or electronic tablet. It's also important to note that as the English language becomes almost mandatory in the global business world, it becomes easier to travel the world and get along with simple English and some basic gesturing---especially in the markets where most merchants know some rudimentary English.

Getting In

Before discussing the ways in which you can get to Cinque Terre, it's a good idea to understand its geography and layout.

Cinque Terre means *five lands* in English, and it refers, of course, to the five villages that make up the region on the Ligurian Coast on the Italian Riviera. In Italy, people refer to the region as *the* Cinque Terre—as in *the five lands*.

The region is comprised of five villages: Monterosso al Mare, Vernazza, Corniglia, Manarola, and Riomaggiore. Trains, ferries and paths connect the villages and car travel here is limited. That is indeed part of its charm.

Here is a breakdown of the five towns:

Riomaggiore — A beautiful, artful mass of pastel houses, and probably the most extensive of the five towns. A cliff-hanging path leads from the beach to old Nazi bunkers and a beautiful hilltop botanical garden.

Manarola has colorful buildings that tumble down a mountain to the harbor. Known for its traditional food and crisp local wine.

Corniglia is mellow, most referred to as "the quiet town" and only one of the five not located on the water. Once departing the train, visitors walk up 400 stairs to this town--located on a hill. This is the town that wine made and it remains so today.

Monterosso is Cinque Terre's resort town with all its modern trappings. Here, you'll find cars, hotels, crowds and a host of bars that make for a lively night-life scene. That's not to say this place isn't charming.

Vernazza is said to be the jewel of Cinque Terre. It boasts a beautiful natural harbor, overlooked by an old castle and church. There are some great restaurants and bars and a street market on Tuesdays.

You can get to Cinque Terre by train, car and ferry, with the most common and practical being the train. Most people depart from Florence, Rome or Genoa or Pisa. If you're coming from Florence or Rome, you'll have to change trains in nearby La Spezia which is on the coast's south tip, or in Pisa.

Travelers coming from Genoa will find a direct train to La Spezia once or twice an hour that stops in Monterosso, and on some schedules Riomaggiore. Depending on where you depart, the trip takes from 1.5 to two hours.

The faster trains are Eurostar (ES), Intercity (IC) or Direct (D). The Regional (R) is a local train that stops in every station. (It's cheaper but slower.)

From points south, take the train to La Spezia, where you must change to a regional train that stops in each one or several of the five towns in Cinque Terre. All of the towns have their own train station. Almost all the trains from La Spezia stop in Levanto. Check your train schedule carefully, though, because schedules vary, and you want to be sure the train you're on stops in the town you are heading to.

When buying a ticket, look for the self-serve ticket kiosk in any station, name your destination, and the earliest time you hope to depart. You will then be given a list of connections and various price points.

You may also want to look into the Cinque Terre Day Pass which allows you to travel all day between the Cinque Terre towns (we'll discuss this in depth further along.)

Train Tips: Since connection times are usually pretty tight, you want to have your luggage in hand and get right off the train when you pull into the station in La Spezia. Also, on the train to La Spezia, sit in one of the first three trains. The train stations are short and the end of the train can sometimes be stuck beneath a tunnel, making it impossible to get off.

Using Riomaggiore as a base, here are the train times to Cinque Terre from various points in Italy:

Pisa --75–95 min. total

Lucca-- 1:30–2 hr. (with a change at Viareggio)

Florence—2- 3 hours (sometimes with a change at Pisa)

Rome ---4-- 5 ½ hours

There are several good websites to help you in planning your train travel to Cinque Terre:

www.trenitalia.com is the official Trenitalia website which will give times and fares for most Italian routes and trains, including sleeper trains, most international trains, and regional trains to smaller places. The English button is a United Kingdom flag at top right. You'll need to use Italian language place names, 'Roma Termini' for Rome, 'Venezia Santa Lucia' for Venice, 'Firenze S. M. Novella' for Florence, 'Napoli' for Naples and so on.

www.italiarail.com is a US-based private agency which sells Trenitalia tickets online in either euros or US dollars, in English and using English-language place names. They charge the same prices as Trenitalia themselves with a small fee. Good site for English speakers.

For a **map** of Italian train routes, see:

http://www.bueker.net/trainspotting/map.php?file
=maps/italy/italy.gif

Buying tickets in advance isn't necessary for regional travel. Pisa to Florence, for example, is considered a regional trek, or Florence to Siena. The only gain from booking ahead is that it saves you a few minutes at the ticket office. There is also no cost advantage to booking early. Purchase your regional tickets at the train station's self-service machine, being sure to validate your ticket at the validation machine before getting on the train. Failure to validate may result in the conductor giving you a ticket on the train and having to pay a fine.

If you're traveling long distances, it's definitely recommended that you purchase your tickets ahead of time. Rome to Florence is considered long distance, or Milan to Venice. Since all the seats on long-distance trains are reserved, it is possible they can be sold out—especially around holidays. Pre-booking also allows you to purchase economy or super-economy fares. If you do buy tickets at the last minute, the base fare will be your only choice.

Driving

While parking is somewhat difficult and expensive, it is possible to drive to Cinque Terre. Remember that the villages don't allow cars in most areas.

There are parking lots at the entrances to several of the villages, but in the summer months they fill quickly. Riomaggiore and Manarola both have small public parking facilities just above their towns and minibuses to carry you and your luggage down. The cheapest option is the big open dirt lot right on the seafront in Monterosso. The priciest is the garage in Riomaggiore. There are hotels in Levanto and some of the other villages that have dedicated parking for cars. Be prepared to pay from 16 to 25 euros a day in the parking lots, or if you find a hotel that allows cars, ask if there is a charge.

Parking Places and Fees

Riomaggiore: 23 EUR/car/day

Manarola: 16 EUR/car/day

Corniglia: 12 EUR/car/day

Vernazza: 12 EUR/car/day

Monterosso: 12 EUR/car/day

Levanto: 9 EUR/car/day

La Spezia - Covered parking near the railway station: 24 euros per day

Driving Route to Cinque Terre

The fastest driving route is via Autostrada A12 from Genoa. Exit onto Corrodano for Monterosso. The trip from Genoa to Corrodano takes less than an hour, while the much shorter 15km (9 1/4-mile) trip from Corrodano to Monterosso (via Levanto) is made along a narrow road and can take about half that amount of time. Coming from the south or

Florence, get off Autostrada A12 at La Spezia and follow Cinque Terre signs.

Be aware that driving from town to town on the mountain pass involves navigating hairpin turns and narrow roads. Be well informed before deciding to drive. You may want to leave your car in Riomaggiore at a paid parking spot and take the train to the other towns.

Ferry

Traveling along the Cinque Terre coastline is a great way to get a different perspective of the villages. The ferries run between La Spezia, Monterosso and Portovenere in both directions. It stops at every village except Corniglia.

Navigazione Golfo dei Poeti runs ferry service to the Riviera towns. While their main purpose is to operate as day cruises, you can ask them to pick you up when you're leaving Cinque Terre.

(www.navigazionegolfodeipoeti.it; (tel) 0187-732-987)

The boats run between April and November. Here are the timetables:

Monterosso - Portovenere

Monterosso: 10:30, 11:35, 12:10, 14:30, 15:00, 16:00, 17:00

Vernazza: 10:40, 11:45, 12:20, 14:40, 15:10, 16:10, 17:10

Manarola: 11:00, 12:40, 15:00, 15:30, 16:30, 17:30

Riomaggiore: 11:10, 12:10, 12:50, 15:10, 15:40, 16:40, 17:40

Portovenere: 11:45, 13:25, 15:45, 16:15, 17:15, 18:10

Timetable La Spezia - Monterosso

La Spezia: 9:15, 10:00, 11:15, 14:15

Portovenere: 10:00, 11:00, 12:00, 14:00, 15:00, 17:00

Riomaggiore: 10:35, 11:35, 12:10, 12:30, 14:35, 15:30, 17:30

Manarola: 10:45, 11:45, 12:20, 12:40, 14:45, 15:40, 17:40

Vernazza: 11:00, 12:00, 12:40, 12:55, 15:00, 15:55, 18:00

Monterosso: 11:15, 12:15, 12:50, 13:10, 15:10, 16:05, 18:10

Plane

There are several options if you plan to fly to Cinque Terre. If you are flying to Italy and looking for an airport close to the coast, you have several options. In the below list you can see how long it takes to get to Riomaggiore by train from your chosen airport. The train usually leaves from the central railway station, so you'll first have to get from the airport to the station. A taxi is your best bet.

Pisa 1–1,5 hours

Genoa 1,5–2 hours

Florence 2,5–3,5 hours

Milan 3,5–4 hours

Rome 4,5–5 hours

Nice 5,5–6 hours

Venice 6,5–7 hours

Getting Around

The most popular way to get around Cinque Terre is by foot. By and large, tourists come to hike the trail between towns. Or they hike to two or three towns and take the train to see the rest.

The most famous network of hiking trails is Sentiero Azzurro, otherwise known as Trail No. 2 or the "Blue Trail." It's made up of four individual paths, and can be walked in roughly six hours. Many hikers spread the route out over a few days, stopping to enjoy the individual towns along the way.

You can start from either direction (Monterosso, heading south, or Riomaggiore, heading north). Perhaps the most practical route would be to start from Riomaggiore. The paths are easier to walk, and largely paved and it allows you time to work your way up to more difficult trails. If you find you're too tired to continue, you can head to nearby train station and get to the next town with ease.

There is a cost to hike Trail No. 2. Depending on the season, it's between 5 to 7 euros a day and also gives access to local museums and an unlimited train pass.

Here is information on the passes for purchase in Cinque Terre from the Go Italy website: (www.goitaly.com)

If you plan only to visit a village but not use any of the connecting paths, you do not need a card. Villages are connected by train or boat and there is a car parking area outside of Riomaggiore. Also when hiking trails connecting the villages (blue number 2 trails) are closed, as is often the case in winter and early spring due to flood damage, cards are not required - ask at the information point.

What's Included with the Cinque Terre Trekking Card:

Use of all pedestrian paths, hiking trails, nature observation points, and picnic areas in the park, except those that may be closed for maintenance. Free map from park offices.

Free access to events put on by the National Park including guided hikes and workshops.

Free use of pay restrooms

Use of public lifts and environmentally-friendly buses that run from each village to points above it.

Free wifi at hotspots in the park.

Discounts on La Spezia museums.

There are a few other trails to tackle in the region if you're game:

The Trail of Sanctuaries: Several paths take you to the area's famous sanctuaries. Some of the paths are challenging, so be sure to have a trail map and talk to tourism personnel before you begin. The paths to the sanctuaries are free.

Mountain Paths: The inland mountain paths are more challenging and frequently appeal to more experienced hikers. Several are free of charge.

Note: Aside from Trail No. 2, the trails between towns can be challenging. It's important to prepare carefully with appropriate footwear, a supply of water and snacks. Dress in layers and carry a daypack,

If you want to spread the hike out over several days, good planning is the key. You can store your bags at a hotel or in the lockers at the train station and bring a daypack with your essentials. It's a good idea to make reservations at a hotel in the villages you intend to spend the night ahead of time—especially in the summer months and holidays.

Train

The trains are a great way to get from town to town, and it's also handy for those that only wish to hike part of the way.

Local trains operate 2 to 3 times per hour between the five towns. Be sure to check the posted train times listed at the station so you'll know what stops your train is making. Some stop only in Monterosso and Riomaggiore. You can buy one-way tickets, or purchase a ticket that is good for 6 hours of travel in one direction. It's a good way to hop from place to place. A day pass is also available that's good for unlimited trips.

Visitor Information

This is your gateway to spending time in Cinque Terre. The tourist office is located beneath the train station in Monterosso (Via Fegina 38. Website: www.turismoinliguria.it) They're open from Easter until September from 9 am to 5 pm. They have reduced hours the rest of the year. It's a good place to get acclimated, and to collect maps and tips.

2 CINQUE TERRE VILLAGES

On the coast of the Italian Riviera lies one of the not so best kept scenic secrets of Italy, Cinque Terre. The town's main villages are closely constructed to one another and by contrast to most of Italy's regions, are rather engulfed by sea, sand and sun as opposed to grand historic architecture. The villages are Monterosso al Mare, Vernazza, Corniglia, Manarola and Riomaggiore.

Monterosso al Mare

Rooted in antiquity, Monterosso is the oldest and the biggest of all the Cinque Terre villages, divided by a single tunnel into two parts, the old town and the new town. It has the best beaches and also the most wine shops, restaurants and hotels. Follow tradition and visit the church of Capuchin Father, from which a breath taking panorama of Cinque Terre can be enjoyed.

Vernazza

Vernazza is the jewel of Cinque Terre, it is visually attractive and picture perfect. Wander the horseshoe-shaped harbor and enjoy a drink or two at Piazza Marconi. The famous walking path that connects the five islands, Sentiero Azzuro, is one trail you do not want to miss in Vernazza. If you grow tired from walking, Doria Castle is your pit stop, built anciently as a watchtower to protect the village from pirates.

Corniglia

Enclosed by two small beaches on each side, Corniglia is the most remote of the five villages and an enchanting terrace. It is a fraction of Vernazza in size, reachable through a flight of steps from the railway station. A well-deserved stop after the climb would be at Gelateria Artigianle for a refreshing taste of Gelato. The beaches are very popular while the wonderful blends of jazz and blues music mix make it worth it.

Manarola

Buildings fall into a step-like fashion in Manarola, as though they are tumbling right into the ocean; the views are astonishing. This village is famous in wine produce from age-old winemaking traditions. Tourists can look forward to winetasting tours through a maze of beautiful vineyards.

Riomaggiore

The village of Riomaggiore is named after a stream that once ran through it; situated within Cinque Terre's National Park, marine life here is breath-taking. There's endless possibilities of water sports on the seashore, food and drinks as well as historic trails such as the Sanctuary of "Madonna di Montenero" and the church of San Giovanni Battista, faceted with marvelous marble doors.

Recommended Walks

Sentiero Azzurro between Corniglia and Vernazza

This is the most popular walking tour in the whole of Cinque Terre. The scenery is an impeccable romantic movie set-up, only ten times more gorgeous.

The Via dell'Amore, from Riomaggiore to Manarola

This trail is known as the Lovers Walkway, simply because you cannot help it but fall in love with Cinque Terre. As you walk in the shade of olive trees, oaks and chestnuts you will see lovers' graffiti inscribed on rock faces, as proof that many have walked this way.

The Trail of Sanctuaries

This is a long stretch of history created after the last war, its title is linked to the fact that it connects all sanctuaries of the National Park of Cinque Terre. On this path the fruits and herbs flourish with abandon.

http://www.parks.it/parco.nazionale.cinque.terre/Eiti.php

3 HOW NOT TO GET LOST IN CINQUE TERRE

Getting lost in a foreign city happens to the best of us, the rest of us, and the most seasoned of travelers. Fortunately most of the streets in Cinque Terre are closely knit with stairways and narrow alleys that always lead back to the main buildings and train stations in each town.

Monterosso al Mare is your main base in Cinque Terre; here you will find more services than in any of the villages. A popular landmark in Monterosso is the main square, Piazza Garibaldi. There's also a tiny tourist info office based at the railway station. Upon exiting the station you will go through a tunnel and either make a left turn for the old town or a right turn for the new town. St. John's Bell Tower can also be used as a landmark as it dominates this town' skyline.

Narrow alleys called "caruggis" branch out from both sides of via Roma, which is the main street in Vernazza, they will take you right back into the village's main hotels and restaurants. Facing the harbor and main street is Piazza Marconi, which may also be used as a central point. A tourist Info

Centre can easily be accessed at the train station.

Corniglia is so small that if you don't slow your steps you can easily go from one end to the next in just 5 minutes. The heart of this town is its main square, the Largo Taragio; you won't miss the many cafes under the large number of trees on this part of town. The town's tourist info center can also be found at the train station, another key landmark to use in finding your way is the Parish Church of San Pietro, which stands next to the village's main square.

When it comes to Manarola, the buildings overlook each other on the main street, via Discovolo; you can easily orientate yourself by this street to find your way if you are lost. Piazza Papa Innocenzio is the town's main square, centrally located and quite easy to find; there's also a tourist information Centre at the train station.

In Riomaggiore's Piazza Rio Finale, you will find a tourist info center, open daily from 9:00am to 10:00pm. Right on the harbor is the town's main Piazza, A Pie de Ma, which can also be used as a landmark if you happen to get lost.

Generally, all tourist information centers across Cinque Terre are open between 9:00am and 10:00pm daily. All travel cards purchases to move around and within the towns, whether by train bus or boat, can be made at each railway station.

4 CINQUE TERRE DAY 1

Riomaggiore. Photo by <u>François Philipp</u>

There is an endless number of ways to explore Cinque Terre and a slew of factors will determine where you stay and what your daily activities will be. If you're hiking, you may want to stay in the northernmost town to take the hike from north to south—the easiest route. Hikers who plan to stay overnight in towns along the way will have to research and plan their itinerary based on their physical ability and preferences. This itinerary is for the traveler who wants to use one hotel as a home base and explore different towns each day.

Day 1

Cinque Terre is about taking it easy. You don't go there to rush from place to place. You go there to laze about and slowly unpack the days.

A good home base is Riomaggiore. It's one of the largest of the five towns and acts as the region's unofficial headquarters. It's the southernmost and easternmost and boasts great charm. It's also where the famous coastal hiking path begins-- the Blue Path.

Pastel and peeling row houses tumble down a steep hill that leads to a small harbor. A good collection of restaurants and bars abound and it's nice to just sit and watch the fishermen come in from a day at sea. You'll no doubt notice a fishing fleet in Riomaggiore that leaves at night to fish for anchovies, using bright lights in the water to attract the fish.

You must also visit the ancient stone castle in town, about which very little has been written. It appears to have been written about in the mind-500's AD, and even then it was described as ancient.

Most of the action in Riomaggiore is on the main street, Via Colombo, where there is an assortment of cafes, bars, restaurants, and of course, sweet shops selling gelato. Small markets sell fresh fruit, an assortment of salami, cheese and olives---great things to stock up on for your hikes.

After checking into your hotel, get right into the mood by having a crisp glass of wine at **Pie' de**

Ma'. Take the stairs at the train station, and head down Via dell' Amore---a three minute walk.

Via dell' Amore. Photo by Jim Rosebery

This is a truly classic place to enjoy an hour or two with a glass of white wine or the specialty from this area called Sciacchetra—a wine made from dry grapes that grow along the beautiful hillsides.

This sweet wine is central to the identity of the region, and the winemaking tradition has been passed from one generation to another here. Pairing Sciacchetra with dessert or cheese is the perfect way to enjoy it. To the people along the coast, it's not just a liquid—it is living history. They believe the spirit of the region lives within each bottle and also represents the hard work that their families endured for generations to sustain their economy and preserve the family winemaking tradition.

Maturing grapes in a vineyard. Photo by <u>Shann Yu</u> CC-BY-ND

A great activity while you're visiting is to visit one of the towns' wineries. If you're lucky you might run into a winemaker along the hiking paths who might be willing to part with a bottle or two of their Schiacchetra wine. But be prepared to pay a steep price. Just one half of a liter will cost $40 or more. There's a reason for the high cost: It takes 45 pounds of fresh grapes to make the 15 pounds of dried grapes needed to extract just one single bottle of Sciacchetra. And then the wine must age for at least 6 years. A very good bottle may have been aged from anywhere from 10 to 30 years.

If you happen to be visiting during the harvest season in September and sometimes October, you'll notice parts of the trail are overrun with wine makers. Harvesting is done by hand because it's too difficult to get machinery into the hills. Vineyard workers used to transport the wine in wicker baskets for miles up and down the hills, but today they use miniature cog-wheel monorails that run along the hills and stop at collection points.

Head down to the marina after you enjoy your glass

of wine to watch the sun sink over the harbor. Sunsets here are world famous. A great place to enjoy dinner is **La Lanterna** on Via S. Giacoma. It overlooks the marina and serves comfort food in a beautiful stone interior.

Today might be a good night to linger over dessert and plan the days ahead. In addition to the itinerary provided here, there are a plethora of good tours to consider, including walking tours, wine tours, boat tours and historic tours. There are local tour companies that combine some of these activities into a single day.

If you're looking for a nightcap after dinner in Riomaggiore, Via Giacoma has a few cafes lining its streets where you can stop in for a cappuccino or a glass of sweet wine.

5 CINQUE TERRE DAY 2

Manarola. Photo by <u>Alberto Carrasco Casado</u>

Today is the perfect day for exploration and getting to know a few of the other villages that make up this unique region. Wear your hiking boots today and bring some water along.

A note about breakfast: A stay in an Italian hotel usually includes some sort of small continental breakfast with cappuccino. If you're looking for something more substantial, head to the nearest café to find more selection.

Bar O'Netto in Riomaggiore is a great spot for a cup of cappuccino and a fresh pastry. Then head back to the train station and up the stairs to make your way to the Walk of Love—or The Via Dell' Amore—the first steps on the famous path.

The Via Dell'Amore path is much more than a hike---it's a journey into history. The path itself winds along the coast on cliffs that look out over the sea boasting unforgettable scenery.

The history of the Via dell'Amore began with the construction of the railway between Genoa and La Spezia in 1926. The path aided in the railway's construction, and later was used as a road. It was the tourists that made the path famous and named it Via dell'Amore—or the road of love. Salt and time have had their way with the old road and today, it frequently closes for repairs.

Walk 1.2 kilometers to Manarola, thought to be the oldest of the Cinque Terre towns. You'll leave the path at the town's train station.

Manarola is a place of grape vines, sweet wine and medieval relics and makes for a great morning stroll. It's all very easy to see as the town consists of one main street.

Manarola. Photo by Alessio Milan

Check out the tiny harbor with its boat ramp, surrounded by picturesque buildings and a great swimming hole if you're game. You won't find a classic beach here, but there's a nice little place to have a deep-water dip, complete with a ladder by the rocks and even an outdoor shower.

The town square here is known as Piazza Capellini. It's a newer addition to the town—built in 2004 but it's a nice place to rest your feet.

It's back to the path now for a hike from Manarola to Corniglia. It's just over a mile and will take you about one to two hours depending on your pace. This is a bit more challenging, largely uphill at the beginning and with a series of steps. If this isn't something you're up for, you can always take the train from Manarola to Corniglia. But if you stick it out, you'll enjoy the astoundingly beautiful scenery on this leg of the hike.

Corniglia. Photo by Pank Seelen

Perched high above the sea, Corniglia is surrounded on three sides by picturesque vineyards and terraces and has beautiful views of the sea to its west. Of all the Ligurian towns, Corniglia is considered the quietest. But it's a great place to stop for lunch.

When you walk through the town, you'll see that the main road leads you through a cluster of lovely homes and interesting shops. If you're there in the fall, the smell of grapes as they're being harvested will fill the air, and having a glass of their famous wine will be an added treat.

Have lunch at the Er Posu Café. The food is locally sourced (with exceptions) and delicious and reasonably priced. Of course, you want to be careful if you're hiking but as a side note, this place has memorable mojitos---made from local limes and mint.

The Gelateria on Via Fieschi has really good gelato

and their specialty will make a great desert—ice cream made with local honey. Anyone who has been to Cinque Terre remembers this Gelateria.

At this point, you can walk down the hill to the train station (a series of 400 steps!) to catch the train back to Riomaggiore. You can also catch a free minibus down the hill to the train station which runs regularly throughout the day.

Corniglia Railway Station. Photo by NH53

Since the towns are so quickly linked by train, be adventurous for dinner tonight if you'd prefer to eat in a town other than Riomaggiore. On the other hand, it might be great to stroll through town and look for a place to watch the sunset and enjoy a light meal before heading back to your hotel.

6 CINQUE TERRE DAY 3

Monterosso. Photo by ccharmon

The itinerary is designed to take you through each of the five towns, so today we'll visit the last two on the list.

Take the train from Riomaggiore to Monterosso this morning after grabbing a quick biscotti and a latte for breakfast. There's a bit of hiking involved for the eager, or feel free to take the train today if you'd prefer.

Monterosso is the last of the five towns and the northernmost and westernmost. It's known as the "resort town" of Cinque Terre and is famous for its lemon trees and anchovies. It also sports a real sand beach. (The sand is more pebble-like and is not fine sand.)

It will seem a great deal busier than the other towns you've visited thus far, but it is still quite charming. Suffice to say, if you are in need of modern conveniences or supplies, the village provides you with ample opportunity to shop today.

Monterosso is actually two towns. The first is the bustling Old Town built behind the harbor, and the second is a relaxed resort that stretches along the beach. There's also a famous treasure housed in the nearby Convento dei Cappuccini, which rests on a hill in the center of town. It's a painting by Anthony van Dyck, the Flemish master who once painted in Genoa.

Church of San Francesco, Monterosso al Mare, Italy. Photo by _Lisa Elliott_

If you bring a beach bag, this morning would be a good time to rent a chair with an umbrella and simply sit near the sea with a good book and enjoy the view. Those visiting in colder seasons might enjoy a walk on the beach.

If you're up for a strenuous walk, head up to the **Church of San Francesco** with its beautiful views and interesting cemetery.

Another opportunity you'll find in Monterosso is a scenic boat tour. Try **Angelo's**, who by all accounts, has a magical tour of the coast which includes appetizers, lunch and when possible, a stop for gelato. It's a great trip for people of all ages—especially enjoyed by kids. (Address: Via Fegina 3)

Walk through **Old Town** by going through the underground tunnel. You'll find plenty of cafes, shops and restaurants there and architecturally and historically interesting churches.

In the foothills above town you'll find a lovely winery called **Buranco Agriturismo**. It's a steep walk but worth the effort for a sampling of wine and appetizers. Ask for a taste of their limoncello—a speciality of the region. (Address: Via Buranco 72)

Make sure to get a map at the tourist office for other things to see and do in this busy town. There are statues, monuments and towers to explore. It's tempting to make a day of it, but don't leave out the last town of Vernazza. It's truly a jewel on the coast.

Vernazza Harbour. Photo by <u>Jason OX4</u>

If you have the time, you can certainly hike the path to Vernazza, but if you're short on time take the train. Walking will involve paying for a pass (or using the pass you bought the first day) and also a bit of step climbing at first. Hikers say the path is challenging at first but gets easier along the way.

In this tiny town of 600, you'll find car-less glory and the only natural harbor in the region. This was once a place where fishing flourished, but the fleet has decreased over the years.

There are some wonderful things to explore here: an old castle where the locals watched for pirates, a historic harbor church, endless vineyards and terraces, and wonderful spots for relaxing.

This is the place for a lovely dinner.

The restaurant **Belforte** is located in a 1,000 year-old tower and depending on the weather, you can sit inside to enjoy the beautiful stonework or outside to enjoy a view of the sea. (Address: Via

Guidoni, 42)

Make your way back to your hotel taking the train tonight.

Santa Margherita d'Antiochia, Vernazza. Photo by <u>Pank Seelen</u>

In addition to the listed activities in the itinerary, here's a list of other recommended adventures:

Swimming – The blue waters are too tempting to turn down a swim.

Go kayaking – Dramatic cliffs, Kool-Aid blue waters makes for a lovely kayak ride along the shore.

Go birding-- Torre Guardiola is a bird watching center and nature observation center just southeast of Riomaggiore marina on Fossola Beach. Lots of flora and fauna to see here and beautiful birds flying about.

Have a picnic-- Shop around town for some local specialties. Restaurants also offer take-out food. Then head to one of the beaches for a lovely lunch and a day of swimming.

Chiesa di Santa Margherita—Head to this picturesque harbor to people watch and relax. The gothic church, Santa Marghertia di Antiochia is here. It was originally built in 1318 and still has an intact bell tower.

Visit the Museo delle Cinque Terre Antiche – Located in Riomaggiore, this small history museum showcases the everyday life of the region. Entrance is free with the Cinque Terre Card.

Visit the churches – Every town along the Cinque Terre has its own collection of churches, which vary in age and architectural style. Take a peek inside the Church of San Lorenzo (Manarola), Santa Margherita di Antiochia Church (Vernazza), or San Pietro (Corniglia), for example.

The Technical Naval Museum is located in La Spezia. The collection is on two levels and showcases the history of Italian naval history and warfare.

7 LOCAL CUISINE IN CINQUE TERRE

Cinque Terre isn't just beautiful, it also boasts with some of the best dishes in Italy. The cooking styles vary from simple grills, to delightful soups, hearty stews and saucy seafood pastas. Fish, olive oil, pesto and wines are symbolic of local traditions.

The Liguria Region is well known for its delicious breads such as focaccia and by no surprise this bread has made its way around the world. It is simply delicious, whether on its own, dipped in sauce or with a spread. The bread is flattened out like pizza and served best when it is hot. Panicia and Farinata are also regular breads, made from chickpea flour and seasoned best with flavorings such as rosemary or onions.

Legend has it that minestrone soup was invented in this area, although we cannot be certain whether it is true or not but the story speaks of soldiers from Genoa that served in the First Crusade making a meal by taking vegetables and herbs from the locals then cooking them as soup in their army helmets. The soup has since been famous; it is hearty and thick, and best enjoyed on cold days.

The Trofie is also a local delicacy; it is a type of

pasta made from chestnut or wheat flour and enjoyed best by adding in squid, lobster, shrimp or razor clams and vangole. Rice and vegetable pies are also among the list of quick bites in Cinque Terre; a tiny crust is stuffed with a mixture of local herbs and rice or vegetables which are then combined with egg and ricotta cheese or béchamel sauce. An excellent choice for a vegetarian!

For adventurous eaters, Genovese is a traditional specialty that involves stuffing a breast of veal with artichokes, peas, breadcrumbs, cheese, eggs, bone marrow and udder. Also typical of the area are gastronomic delights such as stewed cuttlefish, stuffed calamari, spiced octopus and gelato. As a seafood lover, you'll soon be spoilt for choice!

All the grape vines and lemon trees are put into great use; grapes go into producing both red and white wines, such as the famously sweet Sciacchetra (shar-cat-tra) made from dried grapes. The lemons are squeezed into tangy limoncello (lee-mon-chello).

Some of the desserts and confectionaries are violently sweet; one can indulge in Meringhi Genovesi ,a cake soaked in rum or another liquor, filled with apricot jam and topped with vanilla meringue; or Ravioli Dolci, which is an envelope of sweet dough filled with a pesto of citrus, candied squash and citron. On a lighter note, Pacciugo is a combination of bitter chocolate and whipped cream, fresh fruit, cherries and a coulis of raspberry or strawberry.

Recommended Food Tours/Cooking Classes

Cooking Lessons with iL Ciliegio Restaurant

Master the craft of cooking Italian cuisine through classes offered by a popular family restaurant situated atop the beautiful town of Monterosso.

http://www.ilciliegiocinqueterre.com/

Cinque Terre Wine Tour in Riomaggiore

Opt for one of the many wine tours in beautiful vineyards coupled with scenic views, that makes for a relaxing tasting of locally produced wines.

8 WHERE TO DINE

Restaurant on sea wall. Photo by Lee & Chantelle McArthur

There's certainly a list of things you must sample in Cinque Terre—the local specialties that they offer that let you feel as if you tasted the region while you were there:

Anchovies---Don't like them? You may like them here.

Pesto—This region is the birthplace of pesto.

Stuffed Mussels

Sciacchetra-The sweet wine made in this region.

Gelato—Always a must-do anywhere in Italy!

Tegame alla Vernazza--The most typical main course in Vernazza: anchovies, potatoes, tomatoes, white wine, oil, and herbs.

Antipasti

Pansotti ---Ravioli with ricotta and spinach, often served with a hazelnut or walnut sauce

Seafood

Focaccia—A Ligurian bread that has made its way around the world.

Dining out in Cinque Terre can be an expensive endeavor. A restaurant meal generally costs between $25 to $40 USD for a meal with drinks. Remember, too, that most restaurants open for lunch, close for siesta, and then open again around 7 pm for dinner.

For cheaper meals, focus on paninis and pizzas. Wine can be purchased in stores for around $5 a bottle. And there's always a picnic. Run around town and assemble some goodies to enjoy on the beach.

Most Italians eat a quick breakfast of latte and a pastry for breakfast because they're accustomed to having their main meal in the afternoon. You are not going to find a lot of restaurants serving American fare for breakfast. You're going to have to eat like an Italian and find a good coffee shop where you can enjoy a biscotti or a breakfast roll. Many food establishments open their doors at 9 am, and serve latter and lighter breakfast fare.

And like the Italians, you can have a more substantial meal in the afternoon. Dinners are usually late-evening affairs and lighter than the midday meal.

The recommended restaurants included below are not grouped by price, but more by location. Since most substantial meals are priced in the $25 to $40 range, assume the restaurants below fall into that range unless otherwise noted.

Beyond the restaurants mentioned in the three-day itinerary, here are some local standouts:

Lunch or Dinner:

Ristorante Miky in Monterosso. They're known for their grilled calamari. (Address: Via Fegina, 104)

Ristorante La Lampara Ciak in the old town of Monterosso. Try the risotto ai frutti di mare. (Address: piazza Don Minzoni, 6)

Ciliegio in Monterosso al Mare is a great place for seafood. Ask for a plate of trofie made of short pasta twists in an herb-rich swordfish-and-tomato sauce. (Address: Localita' Beo 2)

Fornaio Monterosso has fantastic focaccia straight out of the oven in the mornings and afternoons. (Address: Via Fegina, 112)

Cappun Magru in Casa di Marin is in the village of Groppo, which is a bit above Manarola.

They offer modern Ligurian food, but it's rooted in traditional ingredients and all sourced locally. They're usually just open for dinner. Considered to be one of the best restaurants in Cinque Terre. (Address: Via Volastra 19)

Trattoria dal Billy in Manarola has fresh seafood and astounding views of the terraced hills below. (Address: Via Aldo Rollandi, 122)

Gambero Rosso in Vernazza takes its pasta and seafood seriously and has an enchanting location, right on the quay. Highly recommended (Piazza Marconi 7)

Il Pirata delle Cinque Terre in Vernazza is reasonably priced and owned by a pair of entertaining brothers. The lasagna Bolognese is recommended. Open for breakfast. (Address: Via Gavino 36)

Ripa del Sole is Riomaggiore is a lovely spot with refined food and a nice presentation. Locals love it. (Address: Via de' Gaspari 282)

9 BEST PLACES TO UNWIND

White wine at sunset. Photo by Jérôme Decq

Cinque Terre is not exactly known for its nightlife scene, but there are a handful of bars and clubs in each village.

Manarola: **Cantina dello Zio Bramante** hosts live music on the weekends and is frequented by locals. (Address: Via Renato Birolli 110)

Riomaggiore: You can't go wrong being cliff-side at the **Pie' de Ma' Wine Bar**. The drinks are very good here, and the wine list is impressive. And the view? Indescribable. (Address: Via dell'Amore, 55)

Enoteca da Eliseo in Monterosso is great for snacks and drinks and has a warm atmosphere and a friendly staff. (Address: Piazza Giacomo Matteotti 3)

La Cantina del Pescatore in Monterosso is a nice place to have a glass of wine and check your email. Free Wi-Fi. (Address: via V Emanuele 19)

Bar La Conchiglia in Riomaggiore provides seaside views near the harbor and is a great place to catch the sunset. (Address: 149 Via San Giacomo)

10 WHERE TO STAY IN CINQUE TERRE

Homework. Photo by <u>*Katri Niemi*</u>

Hotels

$$$$

Eremo di S. M. Maddalena—Nestled in the hills above Monterosso, this exclusive hotel was once a hermitage. It boasts a beautiful swimming pool with views of the sea and lovely converted bedrooms make for a relaxing stay. The price even includes a scooter to help you get around town. (Website: www.lamaddalenacinqueterre.it)

La Torretta—Located in the historic center of Manarola, this boutique hotel occupies a tower, meticulously restored to its original 17ᵗʰ century architectural features. (Website: torretta@cdh.it)

La Sosta di Ottone III—Just outside of Cinque Terre in the village of Chiesanuova this beautiful inn is the perfect combination of old world charm and contemporary comfort. The rooms are lavishly decorated. (Website: www.lasosta.com)

$$$

Hotel Porta Roca---The amazing scenery alone makes this a great place to call home in Cinque Terre. Most rooms have balconies overlooking the sea in Monterosso with custom furnishings and a host of other amenities.

(Website: http://www.portoroca.it)

Hotel Palme in Monterosso is just a 2 minutes' walk from the public sandy beach. Offers computer access, a bar, satellite TV and an included breakfast. (Website: Hotelpalme.org)

Appartamenti e Camere Edi is close to the Castle of Riomaggiore and the beach. All seven guestrooms have kitchenettes and daily housekeeping.

(Website: www.appartamenticinqueterre.net/)

$$

Cinque Terre Residence—A great place to

relax—located on a hill set above Riomaggiore. It's a B&B-style inn with modern amenities. Rooms are set in adjoining houses on a terraced hillside. Nice patios with an even better view. Some rooms have kitchenettes.

Pasquale is a fine mid-range hotel with water views from every room. The rooms are fairly small but are decorated with flair. Bathrooms are also small with showers only.

(Website: http://www.hotelpasquale.it)

11 CINQUE TERRE TRAVEL ESSENTIALS

For the final touches to your travel check-list, be sure to add and familiarize yourself with the following essentials:

Currency

The official currency of Cinque Terre is the Euro. You will be able to exchange your money to the local currency upon arrival; exchange desks are located in all tourist hotspots like the airport and train stations throughout Cinque Terre. Another alternative to exchanging money would be inserting your bank card in any of the ATMs to withdraw local money. If you don't feel comfortable with carrying cash on you, a lot of places will accept MasterCard and Visa credit cards. However keep in mind that for small purchases like coffee, breakfast etc., you will need to pay in cash as most business owners will often be reluctant to accept card payments on such small purchases.

Phone Calls

Calling Cinque Terre landline from the United States/Canada:

Dial **011** (exit code) followed by **39** (country code for Italy) then **0187** (Cinque Terre area code) before finally dialing the **local number**.

011 + 39 + 0187 + local number

Calling Cinque Terre mobile from the United States/Canada:

Dial **011** (exit code) followed by **39** (country code for Italy) then the **mobile number**.

011 + 39 + local number

Calling Cinque Terre landline from Europe/Globally:

Dial **00** followed by **39** (country code for Italy) then **0187** (Cinque Terre area code) before finally dialing the **local number**.

00 + 39 + 0187 + local number

Calling Cinque Terre mobile from Europe/Globally:

Dial **00** followed by **39** (country code for Italy) then the **mobile number**.

00 + 39 + local number

When calling from Cinque Terre to another country you will simply dial the Italian international prefix (00) followed by the code of the country you are calling.

oo + country code + area code + local number

Local calls within Cinque Terre

Landline: **Dial 0187+ local number**

Mobile: **Dial 39 + mobile number**

Standard Mealtimes

The standard breakfast of Italy consists of a cup of coffee and sweet baked good; and Cinque Terre is no exception. Breakfast is typically eaten between 7:30am to 09:30am. Lunch is generally the main meal of the day between 12:00pm to 2:30pm. Most restaurant kitchens are closed between 3:00pm and 6:00pm, then open for dinner from 7:30pm until late.

Business Hours

Most public offices and banks are open for business from 8:30am to 19:30pm, Mon-Fri, Sat from 8:30am to 1:30pm and closed on Sundays. The National Park offices are open from 9:00am to 12:00pm and 12:30pm to 6:30pm Mon-Sat, and then open from 9:00am to 12:00pm on Sundays. Everyday shopping hours in Cinque Terre during winter are from 10:00am to 1:00pm, then 2:00pm to 5:00pm. In summer the shopping hours are from 10:00am to 1:00pm, then 2:00pm to 8:00pm.

Key Closure Days

On the following public holidays: 17th of June, 14th of August, 24th and 30th of December, all banks are closed.

Most churches and monumental sites are closed on the following religious holidays: Easter Monday, All Saints 'Day on the 1st of November, Immaculate conception day on the 8th of December and Christmas Day on the 25th of December.

All public and religious holidays are not transferred over if they fall on a weekend.

Lastly, remember that Cinque Terre's climate is the most hospitable in the world, with a general pattern of warm, dry summers and mild winters. You can certainly afford to travel light.

12 TOP THINGS TO DO IN CINQUE TERRE

Cinque Terre's natural and cultural wonders are centered on swimming and hiking. Each little town fills a ravine with a lazy hive of human activities to choose from. Here's our list of 20 things not to miss while in Cinque Terre.

The highlight of any trip to Cinque Terre is the exorbitant **Sentiero Azzuro** path. The path is a stretch of gasp inducing views of the sky and sea between Corniglia and Vernazza.

For a rejuvenating caffeine hit, atop the glorious hills of Vernazza, visit **Bar Matteo's** for the best espressos to date. Address: Via Fieschi, 157, 19018 Vernazza SP, Italy

Castle A. Doria is the remains of the pre 11th century fortifications standing on an impressive hill, silhouetting Vernazza. Its walls are built of rare stones. Open from 10:30am to 5:30pm

http://www.vernazza.ca/attractions/doriacastle.ht
ml

Looming over Monterosso's harbor is the **Torre Aurora Tower** (Tower of Dawn); it is the tallest watchtower to have survived in this town, built by the Republic of Genoa to protect it from pirates.

http://www.lecinqueterre.org/eng/arte/manasanlo
renzo.php

The Sanctuary of **Nostra Signora della Salute** is perched high in the hills of Manarola, dating back to the 10th century. This spiritual path is deemed to calm even the most troubled of souls.

Take pleasure in the historic **Sanctuaries Way** hiking trail. This path connects all the villages' sanctuaries to which each village is attached by deep devotion and pride in heritage.

http://www.parks.it/parco.nazionale.cinque.terre/
Eiti.php

This small nucleus of houses, located above Manarola in **Groppo**, deserves a visit due to the presence of a winery where it is possible to taste and buy the typical products of the Cinque Terre, among which are the celebrated Cinque Terre and

Sciacchetrà DOC wines.

http://www.inmanarola.com/groppo-cinque-terre/

The **Nudist beach**, also known as the Guvano beach is enclosed between Corniglia and Vernazza. This is the unaltered side of Cinque Terre where you will find the bold and the nude.

Have lunch al fresco at the **Borgo Antico Piazza**. The food is unadorned and the wines compliment the menu. Open from 12:00pm to 2:30 pm; 6:50pm to 9:40pm

http://www.borgoanticorestaurant.com/

Il Gigante is the bomb ravaged remains of a colossal Neptune, this unique sculpture is art at its best and an ornament of Monterosso.

http://www.ilgigantecinqueterre.it/indexeng.html

The **Oratorio dei Disciplinati di Santa Caterina**, dating back to the 18th century, is a marvelous panoramic lookout point of the turquoise waters and olive trees in Corniglia.

The **Church of San Francesco**, is a Capuchin monastery built in the 17th century, housing noteworthy artwork, including a Crucifixion attributed to Van Dyck.

The Church of **San Giovanni Battista** in Riomaggiore, dating back to 1340, still houses many valuable paintings and drawings worth gorging your eyes over.

The Castello is an ancient fortress that is on a sheer cliff overhanging the sea, with admirable ruins far above the historic part of the town of Monterosso.

http://www.castellodicasole.com/cinque-terre

Santa Margherita is home to the most beautiful vineyards and best wines in the Liguria area. Wine tasting is done best in this part of Cinque Terre.

http://www.santamargherita.com/en/

The magnificent views of Cinque Terre are incomparable from the **Laspiaggia Restaurant** in Monterosso.

http://www.laspiaggiahotel.com/

The **San Pietro Church** is one of the most intriguing of monuments in Cinque Terre. It displays a rare juxtaposition of gothic styles.

You haven't experienced the truest essence of Cinque Terre until you have taken a **boat ride**. Angelo's boat tours are by far the best in town.

http://www.angelosboattours.com/

A **kayaking tour** in the late afternoon sun of Cinque Terre is as perfect as Italy gets.

It would be a trip incomplete without snorkeling in the beautiful waters of Cinque Terre. The **marine fauna and flora** is incomparable.

13 ITALIAN LANGUAGE ESSENTIALS

Italian is spoken by around sixty two million people globally and is the official language of Italy and one of the four national languages of Switzerland. Most travelers find it easy to pick up basic Italian because much of the vocabulary is similar to its English counterpart, such as museo (museum), studente (student), generale (general), parco (park), banca (bank) and so forth. Below, you will find a few common Italian phrases which you can use in everyday situations during your travels!

Greetings

Hello! – Salve! (*sAH-lveh*)

Good morning! – Buon giorno! (*bwon zhor-no)*

Good night – Buona notte! *(bwoh-nah noht-the)*

Hi! – Ciao! *(chow)*

Good Evening! Buona sera! (*bwoh-nah seh-rah)*

How are you? – Come sta? (*koh-meh STA?*)

Do you speak Italian? - Parla italiano? (*par-lah ee-tahl-ee-ah-no)*

What is the matter? - Cosa c'è? (*koh-zah cheh*)

Thank you very much – Grazie millie (*graht-zee-eh mee-leh*)

What is your name? – Come si chiama? (*KOH-meh see kee-AH-mah?*)

Where are you from? – Di dov'e sei? *(dee doh-veh seh-ee)*

OK! – Va bene! *(vah beh-neh)*

Directions

Where? – Dove? (*Doh-VEH*)

Where is the bus? – Dov'e l'autobus? *(doh-VEH low-TOH-boos)*

Where is the train? - Dov'e il treno? (*DOH-veh eel TREH-no)*

How do I get to _____ Come si arriva a_____ (*Koh-meh see ahr-REE-vah ah...?*)

Hotel –albergo (ahl-BER-go)

Restaurants – ristoranti *(rees-toh-RAHN-tee)*

Straight ahead – diritto (*dee-REET-toh*)

Street – strada (*STRAH-dah*)

Turn left – Si gira a sinistra (*EE-ree ah see-NEES-trah)*

Turn right – Si gira a destra (*EE-ree ah DEHS-trah*)

Past the – dopo il (*DOH-poh eel)*

Before the –prima del *(PREE-mah dehl)*

North – nord (*nohrd*)

South – sud (*sood*)

East -est (*ehst*)

West ovest (*OH-vehst*)

Please take me to____. Per favore, mi porti a _____ (*pehr fah-VOH-reh, mee POHR-tee ah*)

Stop here, please! – Ferma qui, per favore! (*FEHR-mah kwee pehr fah-VOH-reh*)

I'm in a hurry! – Vado di fretta! (*VAH-doh dee FREHT-tah)*

At the restaurant

I'm a vegetarian – Sono vegetariano/a (*SOH-noh veh-jeh-tah-RYAH-noh/ ah*)

I don't eat beef. – Non mangio il manzo. (*nohn MAHN-joh eel MAHN-dzoh*)

I don't eat pork. – Non mangio il maiale. (*nohn MAHN-joh eel mah-YAH-leh*)

Lunch – il pranzo (*eel PRAHN-dzoh*)

Chicken – il pollo (*eel POHL-loh*)

Fish – il pesce (*eel PEH-sheh*)

Beef– il manzo (*eel MAHN-dzoh*)

Sausage – salsiccia (*sahl-SEET-chah*)

Salad– insalata (*een-sah-LAH-tah*)

Eggs – uova (*WOH-vah*)

Cheese– formaggio (*fohr-MAHD-joh*)

The juice – il succo (*eel SOOK-koh*)

The beer – la birra (*lah beer-RAH*)

Excuse me, waiter? – Scusi, cameriere? (*SKOO-zee, kah-meh-RYEH-reh?)*

Please clear the table. Potete pulire il tavolo, per favore ((*poh-TEH-teh poo-LEE-reh eel tah-VOH-loh, pehr fah-VOH-reh*)

It was delicious. È squisito (*EH skwee-ZEE-toh*)

I'm done. Ho finito (*oh fee-NEE-toh*)

One more, please. Un altro, per favore (*oon AHL-troh, pehr fah-VOH-reh*)

Shopping

Expensive– caro (*KAH-roh*)

I am looking for something cheaper. Cerco qualcosa di più economico (*CHEHR-koh KWAHL-koh-zah dee pyoo eh-koh-NOH-mee-koh*)

OK, I'll take it. Va bene, lo prendo. (*vah BEH-neh, loh PREHN-doh*)

Want to take your Italian a step further?

The internet provides a great opportunity to get to know the Italian language. There are several free sites that can help you navigate your way through some simple phrases and allow you to listen to how Italian is spoken. Try www.oneworlditaliano.com. The BBC also offers a great online Italian course for free with helpful phrases, the Italian alphabet and links to Italian classes and courses. You can find it at http://www.bbc.co.uk/languages/italian/.

CONCLUSION

On the streets of Vernazza, Cinque Terre, Italy. Photo by
<u>*Jason OX4*</u>

Cinque Terre is very compact and easy to navigate
with just 11 miles of coastline within its five tiny
towns, but it certainly packs quite a punch. Even if
you're just there to relax and not to hike its famous
trails, there's plenty to keep you occupied. In the
end it's the food, the views, and the people that
make this place so memorable, and in this, Cinque
Terre doesn't disappoint.

EXPLORE OUR OTHER BOOKS

Below you'll find some of our other popular books on Amazon and Kindle as well. Simply click on the link below to check them out.

3 Day Guide to Berlin: A 72-hour definitive guide on what to see, eat and enjoy in Berlin, Germany

3 Day Guide to Vienna: A 72-hour definitive guide on what to see, eat and enjoy in Vienna, Austria

3 Day Guide to Reykjavik: A 72-hour definitive guide on what to see, eat and enjoy in Reykjavik, Iceland

3 Day Guide to Istanbul: A 72-hour definitive guide on what to see, eat and enjoy in Istanbul, Turkey

3 Day Guide to Budapest: A 72-hour Definitive Guide on What to See, Eat and Enjoy in Budapest, Hungary

If the links do not work, for whatever reason, you can simply search for the title on the Amazon website to find them.

35115029R00044

Made in the USA
Middletown, DE
19 September 2016